Keep On Sewing, Betsy Ross!

A Fun Song About the First American Flag

By Michael Dahl

Illustrated by Sandra D'Antonio

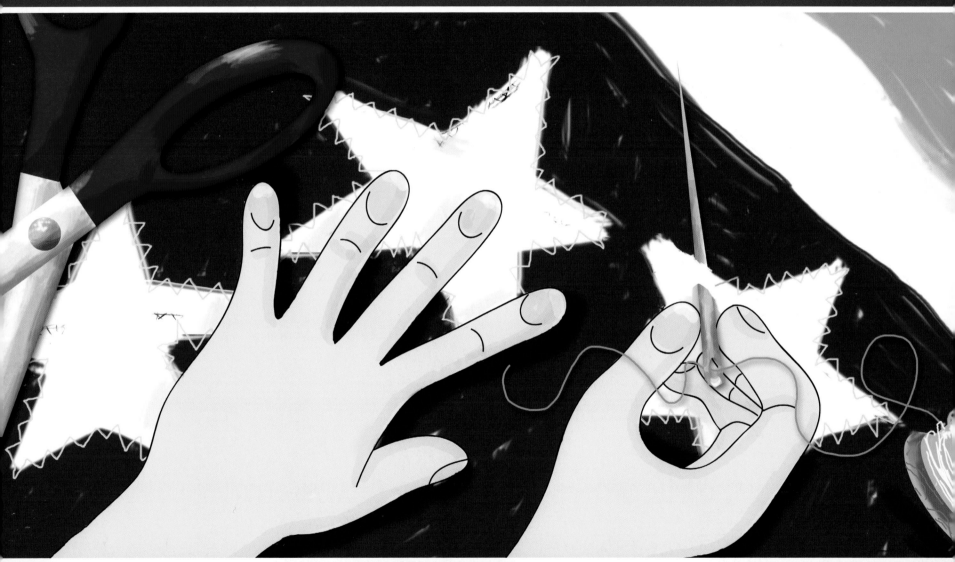

Special thanks to our advisers for their expertise:

Tom Mega, Ph.D., Department of History
University of St. Thomas (Minnesota)

Susan Kesselring, M.A., Literacy Educator
Rosemount–Apple Valley–Eagan (Minnesota) School District

PICTURE WINDOW BOOKS
MINNEAPOLIS, MINNESOTA

Managing Editor: Bob Temple
Creative Director: Terri Foley
Editor: Kristin Thoennes Keller
Editorial Adviser: Andrea Cascardi
Copy Editor: Laurie Kahn
Musical arrangement: Elizabeth Temple
Designer: Melissa Voda
Page production: The Design Lab
The illustrations in this book were created digitally.

Picture Window Books

5115 Excelsior Boulevard
Suite 232
Minneapolis, MN 55416
1-877-845-8392
www.picturewindowbooks.com

Printed in the United States of America.

Library of Congress Cataloging–in–Publication Data
Dahl, Michael.
Keep on sewing, Betsy Ross! : a fun song about the first American flag / Michael Dahl; illustrator,
Sandra D'Antonio.
p. cm. — (Fun songs)
Summary: Relates the Revolutionary War adventures of Betsy Ross, who sewed the first American
flag at the request of George Washington, interspersed with verses of original song lyrics to be
sung to the tune of "Yankee Doodle." Includes bibliographical references (p.) and index.
ISBN 1-4048-0127-8 (lib. bdg.)
1. Ross, Betsy, 1752-1836—Juvenile literature. 2. Ross, Betsy, 1752-1836—Songs and music—
Juvenile literature. 3. United States—History—Revolution, 1775-1783—Flags—Juvenile literature.
4. United States—History—Revolution, 1775-1783—Flags—Songs and music—Juvenile literature.
5. Flags—United States—History—18th century—Juvenile literature. 6. Flags—United States—
History—18th century—Songs and music—Juvenile literature. [1. Ross, Betsy, 1752-1836.
2. United States—History—Revolution, 1775-1783. 3. Flags—United States. 4. Ross, Betsy,
1752-1836—Songs and music . 5. United States—History—Revolution, 1775-1783—Songs and
music . 6. Flags—United States—Songs and music .]
I. D'Antonio, Sandra, 1956- ill. II. Title.
E302.6.R77 D34 2004
973.3'092–dc21   2003009833

SING ONE! SING ALL!
It's the new historical ditty:
"Keep On Sewing, Betsy Ross!"

Sing along to the tune of "Yankee Doodle."
Tell the tale of the first American flag,
made during the American Revolution.
The flag grew with the country!

Long ago, Great Britain's flag flew in America. People there were called colonists. The king of Great Britain was their ruler. The people grew tired of the king's laws. Many wanted to form their own nation. They called themselves patriots. They fought against the British troops.

The patriots wanted their own flag. Their first one was called the Grand Union Flag. Another name for it was the Continental Colors. It had a British symbol on it. But people were confused by that symbol. They thought it meant they were still a part of Britain.

George Washington was the leader of the patriot army. He wanted a new flag without a British symbol on it. George asked a friend to sew the first American flag. His friend's name was Betsy Ross. This song tells the story of that flag.

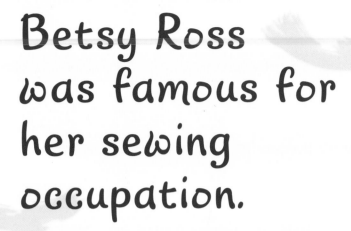

Betsy Ross was famous for her sewing occupation.

Betsy Ross and her husband ran a sewing shop. After he died, Betsy still sewed. She made shirts, dresses, and curtains. She also made flags for ships.

Some folks say she sewed the flag that stood for our new nation.

Betsy told people that George Washington had visited her shop and asked her to sew a new flag. He and Betsy knew each other because they attended the same church.

6

Keep on sewing, Betsy Ross.
Thirteen stars are glowing.

Keep on sewing, Betsy Ross.
Our country's flag is growing.

George did not want the British symbol on the new flag. He wanted 13 stars instead. The stars stood for the 13 colonies.

Betsy Ross's flag was flown
on ships that sailed the ocean.

American sailors used the first flag. They flew it on their ships when they fought the British.

11

When the British saw the flag,
it caused a great commotion.

Keep on sewing, Betsy Ross.
Thirteen stars
are glowing.

After the war, a star was added each time a new state joined the union.

Keep on sewing, Betsy Ross.
Our country's flag
is growing.

Francis Scott Key watched the fight.
The flag flew all night long.

He saw its stars above the bombs
and wrote his famous song.

Francis watched the flag during a British attack in 1814. He wrote a song about what he saw. That song, "The Star-Spangled Banner," became the national anthem in 1931.

Betsy's flag did proudly wave
in calm and stormy weather.

Thanks for sewing, Betsy Ross, the Stars and Stripes together!

Keep On Sewing, Betsy Ross!

Bet – sy Ross was fa – mous for her sew – ing oc – cu – pa – tion.

Some folks say she sewed the flag that stood for our new na-tion. Keep on sew-ing, Bet-sy Ross.

Thir – teen stars are glow-ing. Keep on sew-ing, Bet-sy Ross. Our coun-try's flag is grow-ing.

2. Betsy Ross's flag was flown
   On ships that sailed the ocean.
   When the British saw the flag,
   It caused a great commotion.
   Keep on sewing, Betsy Ross.
   Thirteen stars are glowing.
   Keep on sewing, Betsy Ross.
   Our country's flag is growing.

3. Francis Scott Key watched the fight.
   The flag flew all night long.
   He saw its stars above the bombs
   And wrote his famous song.
   Betsy's flag did proudly wave
   In calm and stormy weather.
   Thanks for sewing, Betsy Ross,
   The Stars and Stripes together!

Did You Know?

Did you know that Betsy Ross might not have designed the first flag? Some people think Betsy Ross did not design the first flag. They think Francis Hopkinson designed it instead. Francis was one of the people who signed the Declaration of Independence. He also designed the Great Seal for his home state of New Jersey.

Francis said he had designed the first flag. He even asked Congress to pay him for his art. Francis was an honest man. No one who knew him believed he would tell a lie. Perhaps no one ever will know who designed the first flag.

Did you know that Francis Scott Key did not see the real battle flag when he wrote his song? Rain was falling during the British attack on Fort McHenry. The leader of the American troops took down the large flag. He raised a smaller storm flag. In the morning, he raised the larger flag. He wanted people to see it from far away. That flag was 42 feet (13 meters) long and 30 feet (9 meters) wide. It weighed 200 pounds (91 kilograms)!

GLOSSARY

colonist—a person who lives in a new land but is ruled by people in a former land

flag—a piece of cloth with a pattern on it; a flag often is a symbol for something

patriot—a person who loves and fights for his or her country

sew—to stitch something together using needle and thread

symbol—a design or an object that stands for something else

To Learn More

AT THE LIBRARY

Duden, Jane. *Betsy Ross*. Mankato, Minn.: Bridgestone Books, 2002.

Ryan, Pam Muñoz. *The Flag We Love*. Watertown, Mass.: Charlesbridge Pub., 2000.

Wallner, Alexandra. *Betsy Ross*. New York: Holiday House, 1998.

ON THE WEB

America's Story from America's Library

http://www.americaslibrary.gov

Offers stories from American history

Betsy Ross Homepage

http://www.ushistory.org/betsy

Tells all about Betsy Ross and her connection to the flag

Fact Hound

Fact Hound offers a safe, fun way to find Web sites related to this book. All of the sites on Fact Hound have been researched by our staff.

http://www.facthound.com

1. Visit the Fact Hound home page.
2. Enter a search word related to this book
   or type in this special code: 1404801278.
3. Click on the FETCH IT button.

Your trusty Fact Hound will fetch the best sites for you!

24